*Justin Isis*

**DIVORCE PROCEDURES FOR THE HAIRDRESSERS OF A METALLIC AND INCONSTANT GODDESS**

Justin Isis has worked as a model, consultant, rapper and visual artist and currently heads the Tokyo Black Lodge occult group. His previous works include *I Wonder What Human Flesh Tastes Like* (Chômu Press, 2011) and *Welcome to the Arms Race* (Chômu Press, 2015). He also co-edited Chômu's *Dadaoism* anthology (2012).

THIS IS A SNUGGLY BOOK

Copyright © 2016 by Justin Isis
All rights reserved.

ISBN: 978-1-943813-04-9

# JUSTIN ISIS

## DIVORCE PROCEDURES FOR THE HAIRDRESSERS OF A METALLIC AND INCONSTANT GODDESS

Snuggly Slim no. 2

天照大御神　　5

Ἔρις　　8

Ἑκάτη　　15

Μηλινόη　　17

觀音　　20

Ἀθάνα　　22

काली　　24

Night　　27

{　}　　28

𓊽𓄿𓀗　　41

# 天照大御神

## 森

Miss Mori's blind green mind forest
encysts spirits like ants in amber. Thought pools
like cool green honey
and sound slips from the cave
when she sings the final name of the sun.

Keep your eyes closed
as you enter the forest,
advancing with your hands. It's not hard
to find the original mouth
whose silence you know already.
Then descend anywhere; some speak
with their hands in the open air,
but I prefer the rising sun
in the wordless world below. To speak
or sing in soundless light
is like fingertips touching a patch of moss.
The damp is aware and awake
and the wind is combing her hair.

Desire beyond these terrestrial commitments
evokes the left-eyed sun.
The air is dancing without depth
and insects sing of the world outside the cave.

## 幽玄

The sun has two moods.
Those who would enter the sun
have two methods: Addition evokes the obverse
through backing away from blindness; the reverse
is reached by singing the darkness of the averse,
averted sun. Subtraction is facing the sun
beneath the ground that rises down,
shining through the dead
as sentimental ghosts.
The blind girl knows that the butterfly
is the most terrible form of that god
who spits in the heart of the sun.

電車

She:

examines her diamond-dusted nails
in an envelope of forestalled extinction.

moistens her lips,
shifts a strand of hair—

the parallel passenger's pocked-potato knees amble inward.

His sunstained shoulders shudder
at those of peach brass: a recognition
of sinking in the same hourglass.

The blind girl brushes away a fly. The eye
-less time that shapes those shoulders
suffers no servants.

# Ἔρις

## Φάρμακον

Consecrated cup
of mescalescent blood and bitter fungal godflesh
chased with the orange dust of the tryptoverse:
Immerse these priests once more in your celestial video
game vistas of ambulant angles and stuttering stars.
It's been too long since that bright isolate crystal
kaleidoscope stained the slides of our childhood,
and we remembered that rainbows can be salted
like slugs until they plump into hot holograms ripe
for our tears to carve
in a style perfect for a midnight tryst
with the Executioner's Daughter
who you can find in a pack of cards
or sitting in the middle of the dancefloor
staring at the ceiling.

> It's been too long since we slipped through the Door in
>     the Wall
> and broke into the gift shop to talk with those bangles
>     and baubles and
> burbling babbling Bubble Bobble dinosaur dragon icons of
> passionate impertinent electric infinity

whose names we can never recall.
Too long since we read the walls at all.
I guess we got distracted by that mission they gave us
about finding the meaning of life. Our research team
    scored the answer
which had something to do with Love, Family and
    especially
showing up to appointed places at appointed times
so capitalism could run smoothly
and Warren Buffett would not have to perform manual
    labor.
There were subclauses about responsible consumption
and not leaving a footprint.
Anyway it was all rubbish
so we've been feeling down,
not wanting to disappoint the Bubble Bobble galaxy
and its tremendous screaming pulsing floral operatic
    metaphor machinery
in case they decide not
to take us off the grid
again.

But remember the silver nymphs without faces?
Ces nymphes, je les veux perpétuer.
It's been too long since we had our lobes lanced
by Lucy aka Lady Lucifer the laser lightbringer
or our minds muddled and mollified
by Molly that's been modified.
We've occupied our time with various glands
and daily reflection on silver and yellow sounds.

黄色は、考え過ぎると病気になりやすいなど悪いイ
メージを持たれがち。
しかし、毎日この色を考えることで健康に良い影響
を与える。
Remember the yellow nymphs without faces?

Das Rätsel dieser Welt löst weder Du noch ich,
Jene geheime Schrift liest weder Du noch ich.
Wir wüssten beide gern, was jener Schleier birgt,
Doch wenn der Schleier fällt, bist weder Du noch ich.

Our marrow has been lost
to hungry clocks. Status updates
from those who have never tasted martyrdom report
that living and thinking like a mobile marketing
    consultant goes hand in hand
with not unduly assassinating forests to save face.
當那些主義經過時違法的彩虹王國就流淚了
Instead, focus on the peacock angel of the inner eye
and the shadows rushing in at its edges.
Moi, de ma rumeur fier, je vais parler longtemps
Des déesses; et, par d'idolâtres peintures,
A leur ombre enlever encore des ceintures:
Ainsi, quand des raisins j'ai sucé la clarté,
Pour bannir un regret par ma feinte écarté,
Rieur, j'élève au ciel d'été la grappe vide
Et, soufflant dans ses peaux lumineuses, avide
D'ivresse, jusqu'au soir je regarde au travers.

Strangled by wireless phones in calendrical cages,
it's been a long time since our last Assumption
into the iridescent essence of the Empyrean Empire
and a long while since we were last abacinated
by those incarnadine incarnations
of little purpureous flowers
emicating explosively.
Too long since we were last abducted by aliens
and cracked jokes in the Chian language before
parachuting back to the haunted suicide forest that
flowered with our own faces.
Remember those timeslipped Orangemen with redcoats
and Roundheads with broadswords?
I think they were really pillow mites with pincers
mounting an eyelid campaign
or ancestral antipathies stranded on Mind's shore of
   morning.
None of us could explain the nymphs
so we put them through the Turing Test
which they passed with flying colors
while waving colored flyers. We had more trouble
with that Hermetic Joker who leaped over Death
and extended himself indefinitely while smiling
from the walls and promising a younger gravity.
Then there was the time
three hours from now
when we danced and crawled on the floor like children
and fed each other red blood oranges
which were red at first and orange after
like the dust drifting through the happenstance hyperspace
that is happening then and now as we are dancing.

Consecrated cup of orange dust and blood red juice:
Immerse these crawling priests in the eternity
since we awoke in timeless infinity and remembered
remembering it eternally;
or in other words
since we awoke in infinite eternity and
remembered remembering it timelessly. In this
and that orange ecstacy, the Joker
and the nymphs are requited
and the angel's
peacock tail
fans from the
inner eye
forever.

## Αχεραλον

Anyway fuck that undepictable desert that verses
hissed by angels have dumped over our garden
of black soil and writhing worms called nerves.
I guess we need some Exterminators at home
despite their track record: Imagine Hubbard's surprise
when the arsenal he'd stolen from Parsons
worked as advertised. We told those virgins
and merchants and other dim bulbs
not to leave their entrails lying around but still
the angels scrabbled through the cracks. I've heard they
can fly but can't imagine anything so terrible.
That hissing sound they make
and the way they dart out so suddenly
is bad enough. I've heard they've got golden plates too
but wouldn't trust the smile of anything that breeds
so quickly in dry places without flowers.
The desert is falling from the sky
and it's hard to have a picnic with sand in your eye.
The fine grains are trouble but the worst are those
big chunks that look like dead cartoonists.
I woke up one night and found an angel in my room—

## 14

"The Word!" it began, but I crushed it with a rolled up
newspaper before it could flash its golden plates
and try to sell me the desert.
If an angel should appear at your picnic,
remember to use the arsenal
which is still black and still writhing,
freely available in any
area of the air.

# Ἑκάτη

Εἰνοδίαν Ἑκάτην κλήζω, τριοδῖτιν, ἐραννήν,
οὐρανίαν χθονίαν τε καὶ εἰναλίαν, κροκόπεπλον,
τυμβιδίαν, ψυχαῖς νεκύων μέτα βακχεύουσαν,
Περσείαν, φιλέρημον, ἀγαλλομένην ἐλάφοισιν,
νυκτερίαν, σκυλακῖτιν, ἀμαιμάκετον βασίλειαν,
θηρόβρομον, ἄζωστον, ἀπρόσμαχον εἶδος ἔχουσαν,
ταυροπόλον, παντὸς κόσμου κληιδοῦχον ἄνασσαν,
ἡγεμόνην, νύμφην, κουροτρόφον, οὐρεσιφοῖτιν,
λισσομένοις κούρην τελεταῖς ὁσίαισι παρεῖναι
βουκόλῳ εὐμενέουσαν ἀεὶ κεχαρηότι θυμῷ.

Astronauts crawl across your face as if the aim of the race were to reach that airless shrine unseen of Spring. The timidity of antiquity enthroned three phases and faces of the Fear in the sky beyond fate; the fourth facet of the fanged fossil virgin fills our inner eyes when night has fallen.

The pillars of your legs rise above the lunar seas; the corpses strewn in offering cast dancing reflections on waves that no one sees. The faces of the dead sink in memory which some call the sea of fertility. Lunacy is looking back when the underworld lies behind; an owl knows to look to the side.

Our Lady of the Grey Desert lowers her mask of bone. Stripped of clouds we glimpse the mouth of her barren womb and hear the name that the crownless dead have spoken. The silhouette of the silent huntress slips from the smoke and stands alone. Only her priests remain: the slaves of the Book are dead and broken.

Desire feeds the wolves of the cardinal crossroads who wear three faces; the fourth cannot be seen and stalks from a different direction. The owl declaims that nothing can be attained by attainment and nothing atoned for by atonement; Nothing is attained when no thing is owned: the priest alone sleeps beneath the moon where desire in its waxing and waning is intoned.

# Μηλινόη

Μηλινόη's face is filthy frozen snow
frosting the iron shores of night.
We pray in praise of the shadows below.

A scarlet candle spreads its glow
to guide our way with spectral light.
Μηλινόη's face is filthy frozen snow:

pale as a dove and black as a crow,
pale as maggots and black as flies in flight.
We pray in praise of the shadows below.

As pallid Moon commences crimson flow,
the Averse Sun expels its ebon light.
Μηλινόη's face is filthy frozen snow.

Her cloak of saffron spreads to show
phantasmal flesh of darkness bright.
We pray in praise of the shadows below.

Our maddened minds melt and flow;
Μηλινόη's face replaces sound and sight.
Μηλινόη's face is filthy frozen snow.
We pray in praise of the shadows below.

Frosting the iron floors of Hell,
Μηλινόη's filth is frozen blood and snow.
The tapeworm nite lite casts its glow

from bottomless Pit to Heavenly height.
Μηλινόη's pallid maggots squirm and bite
in snow-furred corpses rotting slow.

The spectral dove unlaces its arteries.
The Sun in the underworld has ebony thighs.
Μηλινόη eats frozen prayers.

We praise the screaming saffron snow
and fly-blown crows with human eyes in fright.
Μηλινόη's womb is a cemetery of the universe.

Fucking in furred, frozen excrement
in the blacklight theatre of the underworld
feels like being stung by bullets
fired from a machine gun made of skin, bone and hair.

Soundless sightless prayers flutter through the air.
Μηλινόη's white hands and ebony thighs are covered
    with blood.

The machine gun leaks semen and licks our faces.

Filth-furred corpses melt and flow
as pallid Moon fucks the rotting light and chews on the
    faces of the dead.

We pray in praise of Μηλινόη killing every part of us by turning us inside-out so our hearts will be exposed to the light of the Averse Sun in the underworld.

Let our prayers fly as fast as soundless sightless spectral crows with cancerous eyes and feathers encrusted with filth and blood and frozen snow.

We pray in praise of the open saffron robe and phantom flesh changing from black to white and white to black and roiling with blood like a scarlet candle melting in the mouth of a burning corpse.

Μηλινόη's face is pallid ebony and a blinding maggot-white Sun.

Her womb is full of insects and machine guns and we wish only to die while fucking in the heart of the Averse Sun in the underworld.

Μηλινόη's face is filthy frozen snow.

We pray in praise of the shadows below.

觀音

Goddesses are like bats,
perceiving the sounds of the world.
The Maria eunuch factory,
its plaster casts ravenous as rats,
is strapped on like a phylactery,
leaving dreamless girls ungirled.

These catechized commodities weep,
lamenting as the bottle dulls
the ache of a laminate virginity,
vexed to shallow sleep;
while, tolling empty infinity,
tiny nuns circle their skulls.

And manufactured eunuch boys,
strung up in whitewashed tombs,
are stained with smoke from Marian censers.
Rotten with renunciate joys,
their fear feeds sin-starved censors,
carnivorous in confession rooms.

Misery's map is traced by cries;
space itself and time are torn
by every grief our minds can fashion.
One alone and in need relies
on the bodhisattva of compassion,
thousand-armed, lotus-born.

Sorrow echoes, etching ghosts.
From golden thrones and beggars' mats,
觀音 hears fears, appeals hurled;
salves our doubt, endures our boasts.
Perceiving the sounds of the world,
goddesses are like bats.

# Ἀθάνα

## Γλαυκῶπις

Princess priestess
Surgically clean
Inanimate Libra
Mistress Mercury
Embed your thoughts
with closed captioning.
Monitor lizard
Queen of mirrors
Embed your thoughts
within our thoughts.
Surgical priestess
Mother of Memory
Appraising with scales
at the back of the brain.
We strike any key
to continue
until scales fall
from the monitor's eyes.

## Ἀποτρόπαιοι θεοί

Pluripotent plenipotentiary locked in the penitentiary
mothered by matter. Each cell makes many
embers of empire each aeon and century.

Image-inbred instrumentality
of electronic cosmetic surgery:
Arch-imagined imago
draws spectators like a roadside fatality.

Photosapient phantom of wire-lost nights,
Our Lady's lashes grid the world
like a fascist city's sentinel street lights.

Smile poised past a moment of propulsive
polyplasticity. Blogspot posts a bitcropped Leda,
like a bloodied swan sublime and repulsive.

Refuge from evolution's errors,
Tower of Glass, Polymer Rose, Chemical Sea
Lacquer our youth and cleanse our terrors.

# काली

It was easy to enter the world of the Buddha,
much more difficult to undertake the Black Pilgrimage
on a scheduled payment plan
in inclement weather
surrounded by content specialists
gross minor kindnesses
reasonable atheists
one-click ads
and small independent presses.

In early life
my school field trip
to the Black Cathedral
was cancelled due to the clerical errors
of error-prone clerics.
Much later I applied
to undertake the Black Pilgrimage
and was told further study
and preparations were required.
Meanwhile the world of the Buddha
continually spammed my accounts
requesting I like its Facebook page

support its protests
follow its feeds
and fund its old age.

After losing my youth
I set out again for the Black Cathedral
only to learn
that it was undergoing renovations.
I wandered through the black desert
for a thousand years each night
until I came to the place marked on the map
that I had found years before
lily-like
floating and almost dissolved
in a toilet in the little girls' room
that my friend Charles
had dared me to sneak into
before I lost my youth and
when I was still impressed
by the world of the Buddha.
I remember running back to safety
with the dripping page in my hand
and seeing a girl in the mirror
with black shoulders and black hair
and arms propped by crutches
her face turned away
her outline barely there.

Now all that was left of the Black Cathedral
was a tiny room
suspended by crane
above an abyss
its windows boarded up.
I broke in and scrawled
my name on the wall
with a magick marker
and pissed on the floor
before taking these photos
with my iPhone.
Moments later
I awoke in the middle of an Arby's
In Columbus, Ohio
seated before a sandwich
of shaved beef and orange cheese.
It's been three weeks already.
I have no descendants
and my credit is preventing loans
but I was in the Black Cathedral
and remember the laughing face
of the girl with broken bones.

# Night

Nuit
Bodied night
Flesh, starlight
Night-blue fruit
Atomless void:
Hadit, employed
Enamelling shells
Shed from the mind.
Point known never;
Void known, entered from behind
Des Cieux Spirituels l'inaccessible azur,
Pour l'homme terrassé qui rêve encore et souffre,
S'ouvre et s'enfonce avec l'attirance du gouffre.
За радость тихую дышать и жить
Кого, скажите, мне благодарить?

{ }

Drunk at the funeral
with minds and inner mansions dancing,
the most heavily-anthologized dinosaurs
stripped themselves of survival drag:
no scales or feathers
only reflective membranes
clear as the glass of a microwave timer.
Swiping each other's skins like a hookup app:
vaporware dinosaurs
without their military beauty,
tender and reflective.

Meanwhile Mega Man rode on Sun Wukong's cloud,
a Blue Bomber in search of narcotic novelties.
It was easy to get a fillet of fish in the Pure Land
even without a discount voucher.
Seventy-two demons appealed to him
from the corners of everyday life;
fifty-three were above the age of sixty-four
while the remaining nineteen were only sixteen.
Blues were not necessary for the Bomber
although iron and zinc helped.

Exhibits of regret in the mourning museum
attracted a pastel palette: orange blossoms and pink roses.
Deposing the Monkey King
had been like eating a hot iron
he could not spit out.

The hideous unknown
is never as hideous
as the partially known.
Subwoofers blooming in the basement
compelled the consistency of the air
as we held the iron in our mouths
and nineteen demons danced
at the gates of the mourning museum.
Entering the nameless goddess glacially
is mainly a matter of resisting unwanted funerals
that the museum attendants are constantly seeking to
    stage,
while demons under glass
can be deleted with a swipe of the thumb,
except for the ones who call you
when they're drunk and already inside the taxi.
Deposing the hideous unknown
is never only a matter
of caressing each other's skins
in the pastel morning.

Nursing a cold, the Blue Bomber surveyed Stonehenge,
Electronics Boutique, Yugoslavia,
the lost continent of Mu,

the ruins of Hyperborea
and the University of South Carolina.
Sharing drinks with the dinosaurs had been fun
but now it was time for total annihilation.
The Mega Buster was adept at divesting routines
of their consistency
and infesting dynamic systems with entropy;
unleashing it in the bright air felt a little like coughing
after the first cigarette of the morning.

After the collapse
no post-apocalyptic postmen remained
to parcel out the past.
There were no dancing birds
or singing demons
and silence screamed in the mourning museum.

Deposing the known
is never only a matter
of destroying the world.
If Hell is a tiny spot
on a corner of the carpet of Heaven,
then Heaven might be a
stain on the train
of the nameless goddess
who Mega Man imagined
as he floated above the wreckage
of the workaday world
with its naked and dead dinosaurs,
nonexistent postmen

and mourning museums screaming
with the silence of deleted demons:
Her back was turned
but just for a moment
he caught a pinprick flicker
playing about her feet.

Fade out on
any jobless Nightmare Life-in-Death
fixated on the state lottery
and small surveillance changes—
dice, rolled bones, frame adjustments
without much health care
no longer fashionably emaciated
but getting a little soft,
relaxing into the atmosphere
like a snail under rain.

Zoom out on childhood curses
from snaps of the day frozen

in sculptural memory.
Even minor terrors are welcome
in the hotel of me—

occupy space in my body
agitate thoughts of thoughts
as the heartbeat of a moth is
gripped by the heart of a light.

Become present in
self at present
and future self—

sidereal sisters
of or relating to
the back-blinking time machine
unable to catch
some fulfillment
that is already past.

Memorials of the immemorial
a possession taking
orphaned aims;

illustrious noble train
beneath the solid ground retires
as white bounteous ghosts,
microscopic huntresses
cross the rough rock to wander—

(leader and nurse be present to our rites
with broad survey, illumining all the sky.
Self-born, unwearied in diffusing light.)

At half past seven
A maiden on the hillside
looking for seven herbs
in autumn
was observed by the emperor

who had been watching the clock,
counting the minutes,
scanning every form that came along
with the crink-crank-crick through the round stile of
    the pay-gate—
the first blood was, strange to say, his own.

The iron pier was a varied and animated scene.
A young promenading maidenhood
half-danced time with an alternate scrape and stroke
of soles upon the floor—
puffs of tobacco smoke
the revolving light of the lightship in the channel
seen above the flash and flare of the pier lamps
and the water sloshing between the open timbers of the
    pier pavement.

Sometimes the deep rumble of the sea could be heard
over the clash and clang
of earrings upon the air.
In September daylight and darkness are equally divided
but there are other ways of hunting
than by sight.

The marketplace is crowded
With journalistic memory—

Whatever; there's no real history,
or rather
history is fastened onto naked templates
like the job skills
in Final Fantasy V;

alive, we analeptic robbers
ransack tombs
to answer boredom.
The more scrupulous copyists
always get a pass
in applauded,
public
sculptural memory
even though
they're only templates
without Life, Death or Nightmares.

I would rather the emperor
gather his childhood curses
to scour the walls of the tomb,
flapping like an agitated moth
before alighting on sleep
and awakening later,
when the maiden has returned from autumn.

Let their thought divide
against and in spite of its
inherent limits. Spread far
while weakening all the way.
This is to cancer a view.

Let their children spit
out all their certainty like
a mouthful of mold.
Also erode their culture.
This is for 'true believers.'

Tired of those with eyes
only on the registry
office. Bring the mad
and uselessly ambitious.
This is to summon witches.

Whatever was dreamed
before it could be attained
will come without fail,
still necessitous or not.
This is to limit despair.

The blank universe
does not itself applaud us.
Its opinion would
be ignorant anyway.
This is to foreground action.

Catastrophic and unsubtle events
were not occurring
on the LinkedIn comments section
of my cousin the homeless assassin.
Out on the range
there was nothing vacant.
No one was sculpting the astral body of rapture
with the chisel of an exasperated geometry.
Genital crab vampires were not siphoning our fluids
without a warrant
in service of mail order brides
and forbidden clinics.
A naked mannequin covered in moss
was not ladling black honey into paper cups,
and jackal-headed speculators could not be observed
slotting coins in our abandoned anatomies.
There were no altars anywhere.

Countless young men are born dead
in civilized warehouses
with tape decks but no windows.
They loll like doll parts, musical and dismembered,

lyrics resounding in their hollow bones
(milked for martyrdom
in alabaster abbatoirs).
Spiders toss litter and sprinkle glitter.
A pig ventures a critical snout.

The Mushroom Kingdom unleashes its armies,
led by Commander Toad, the intermediary—
glyph face, with a button cap and coins for eyes.
We scribbled his veve at the crossroads
and swore we'd rot in a suit of him.
Mold in the shower conscripted us into service:
Living in illness is living. The next step
is coming forth by day.

Toad gives birth in the Diaryland Library:
His soldiers feed on Books of the Dead
and Books of the Living.
Blackened pages of illegible spells
sprout aberrant commas,
flecked footnotes,
soft wet commentary. The air clenches.
All the sorrow that's fit to print
is fit to feed the spreading guardian of the gate
of life and death.
Dolls with endorsed skills sing sorrow songs
as Commander Toad smokes a Cohiba.

Somewhere a hag is gathering stones,
receipts and blood packets,

Catastrophic and unsubtle events
were not occurring
on the LinkedIn comments section
of my cousin the homeless assassin.
Out on the range
there was nothing vacant.
No one was sculpting the astral body of rapture
with the chisel of an exasperated geometry.
Genital crab vampires were not siphoning our fluids
without a warrant
in service of mail order brides
and forbidden clinics.
A naked mannequin covered in moss
was not ladling black honey into paper cups,
and jackal-headed speculators could not be observed
slotting coins in our abandoned anatomies.
There were no altars anywhere.

Countless young men are born dead
in civilized warehouses
with tape decks but no windows.
They loll like doll parts, musical and dismembered,

lyrics resounding in their hollow bones
(milked for martyrdom
in alabaster abbatoirs).
Spiders toss litter and sprinkle glitter.
A pig ventures a critical snout.

The Mushroom Kingdom unleashes its armies,
led by Commander Toad, the intermediary—
glyph face, with a button cap and coins for eyes.
We scribbled his veve at the crossroads
and swore we'd rot in a suit of him.
Mold in the shower conscripted us into service:
Living in illness is living. The next step
is coming forth by day.

Toad gives birth in the Diaryland Library:
His soldiers feed on Books of the Dead
and Books of the Living.
Blackened pages of illegible spells
sprout aberrant commas,
flecked footnotes,
soft wet commentary. The air clenches.
All the sorrow that's fit to print
is fit to feed the spreading guardian of the gate
of life and death.
Dolls with endorsed skills sing sorrow songs
as Commander Toad smokes a Cohiba.

Somewhere a hag is gathering stones,
receipts and blood packets,

abandoned autographs,
crumbling cigarette butts,
cups of the ocean
and the cores of candy apples.
Reassembler
of the dismembered:
A sun sits in her.

I left my heart lying on the sand,
a plump pump plucked from the place where
catamenial casualties ride on cancer crabs
and the lion chases the ram. The Water-Bearer
drags scales across the abdominal ecliptic
to weigh the menagerie. Ceremonial animals
of the firmament bleed in flame: rat, snake and dragon.
And there are women silhouetted in the seasons,
basket-bearing, sacrificing and sacrificed.
All this in a body, cast to the four corners.

I kept coins for Toad
and his long ferry through the air
(a susurrus of settling spores):
thalers and bobs
a handful of won
and wooden knickels. His army rested
in my remains, supplied itself with spit,
gristle and wishes. Dreams ran rivers
from my empty sockets. A regiment
garrisoned itself in those pools
and erected fat-capped
fruiting towers.

The Throne found the rest of me
in a pile of parts—
shadow refuse from the warehouse
with a half-life measured in kalpas,
universally homeless
but weighing less than a feather.

Sailor Venus in transit,
transgender, transitioning in the warehouse,
sweating over doll boys and Mushroom Men
watched me take shape,

not as mass-produced lyrical horror

or even an identifiable sadness

but as a dance of ceremonial animals
in the sky beneath her feet.

Conscripted into the army,
the Throne stitched me, made me.

Now there are pink altars
and the Throne is careful to beauty.

www.ingramcontent.com/pod-product-compliance
Lightning Source LLC
Chambersburg PA
CBHW020035120526
44588CB00031B/833